Cutting Edge

COOL CAREERS

VIDEO GAME DEVELOPER

By Chris Jozefowicz

Content Adviser: Gabe Newell, Managing Director, Valve Corporation

Gareth Stevens
Publishing

Please visit our web site at **www.garethstevens.com**.
For a free catalog describing Gareth Stevens Publishing's list of high-quality books, call 1-800-542-2595 (USA) or 1-800-387-3178 (Canada).
Gareth Stevens Publishing's fax: 1-877-542-2596

Library of Congress Cataloging-in-Publication Data
Jozefowicz, Chris.
    Video game developer / by Chris Jozefowicz.
        p. cm. — (Cool careers: cutting edge)
    Includes bibliographical references and index.
        ISBN-10: 1-4339-1958-3   ISBN-13: 978-1-4339-1958-9 (lib. bdg.)
        ISBN-10: 1-4339-2157-X   ISBN-13: 978-1-4339-2157-5 (pbk.)
        1. Computer games—Programming—Vocational guidance—Juvenile
literature. 2. Video games—Design—Vocational guidance—Juvenile
literature. I. Title.
    QA76.76.C672J68   2010
    794.8'151023—dc22   2008053549

This edition first published in 2010 by
Gareth Stevens Publishing
A Weekly Reader® Company
1 Reader's Digest Rd.
Pleasantville, NY 10570-7000 USA

Executive Managing Editor: Lisa M. Herrington
Senior Editor: Brian Fitzgerald
Senior Designer: Keith Plechaty
Produced by Editorial Directions, Inc.
Art Direction and Page Production: Paula Jo Smith Design

Picture credits: Cover, title page, Jupiter Images/Comstock Premium/Alamy; p. 5 David
L. Moore—Lifestyle/Alamy; p. 6 David Grossman/Alamy; p. 7 Namco; p. 9 (bottom) Valve
Corp.; p. 9 (top) EA SPORTS; p. 10 Darryl Bush/San Francisco Chronicle/Corbis; p. 13 (top)
Elizabeth Delage; p. 13 (bottom) Graphic Art by David Hellman; p. 14 Christopher J. Morris/
Corbis; p. 15 Donald Bowers/Getty Images for Guiness World Records; p. 17 Ido Magal; p. 18
aberCPC/Alamy; p. 21 RedOctane; p. 22 Associated Press/Ric Feld; p. 23 (top and bottom)
Courtesy of Kyle Gabler; p. 25 ImageSource/Art Life Images; p. 27 Associated Press/
Gautam Singh; p. 28 Associated Press/Elaine Thompson

Printed in the United States of America

1 2 3 4 5 6 7 8 9 14 13 12 11 10 09

CONTENTS

Words in the glossary appear in **bold** type the first time they are used in the text.

CHAPTER 1

WORLD BUILDERS

Y ou've probably already been to outer space. You have driven race cars. You have played professional football. You have rescued princesses. None of this happened in real life, of course. No, you have lived in the amazing **virtual** worlds of computer video games.

The people who create these adventures are called **video game developers**. They are some of today's hottest entertainers, even if you don't know their names.

In 2007, Americans spent more than $9 billion on video games. The business is growing much faster than music and movies. It's drawing in more game developers than ever before.

What Does a Game Developer Do?

Video game developers make video games and the machines that play the games. They create the stories. They craft the sounds and sights. They make the games fun to play.

Game developers write software. Software is the operating instructions and **programs** that a

Video games take their players to virtual worlds. This girl plays video baseball using the Nintendo Wii.

computer uses. Video game software is stored on discs and cartridges. It is also on video game **hardware**.

Hardware is the computer equipment. It includes arcade machines, home gaming systems, personal computers, and game systems that fit in your pocket.

Video game developers create games for arcade machines.

Game developers must stay on the cutting edge of technology. New software and hardware help them make games that are even more fun to play. Developers are always trying to improve the look, sound, and feel of their games.

A Brief History of Video Games

1958: A research scientist produces an early video game called *Tennis for Two*.

1962: College students use a room-sized computer to create *Spacewar*.

1972: Magnavox releases the first home video game system called the Odyssey.

1977: The video game system Atari 2600 comes out. It goes on to sell more than 30 million units.

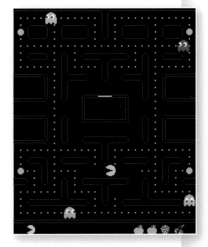

1980: *Pac-Man* (above) chomps his way into arcade machines.

1995: Sony sells the PlayStation in the United States.

2006: Nintendo releases the popular Wii game system.

Is This Career Right for Me?

- Do you like playing games?
- Do you like working with computers?
- Do you like math and **logic** puzzles?

If so, video game developing might be for you. Some game developers start out as artists or electronics **engineers**. Many developers study computers in school. One thing all developers share is a love of computers.

CHAPTER 2

MAKING A GAME

E very video game starts in the same place: the game maker's imagination. From there, different games take different paths. Some games are designed on a personal computer by one game developer. Other games need a big team working on the most cutting-edge equipment.

Game developers have many styles to choose from when they make their games. Some games show characters running and jumping. Others let players look through the eyes of their character. Some games look very realistic, while others are cartoonish. The vision for a game often helps a developer choose the tools needed to make it.

The Design

Many game makers say that designing the game is the hardest part of the job. Game developers must ask many questions before programming starts. Will the game ask players to follow a single path to victory? Will players have many choices and ways to win? Will the game look true to life or out of this world?

Players of *Tiger Woods PGA Tour 09* (above) watch their character in action. Players of *Portal* (below) look through the eyes of their character. Game developers choose how players see the game.

Many talents are involved in the making of a game. Artists may craft **concept art** to guide the look of the game. Concept art shows the design or mood of a video game before it is used in the final product. Writers may add to the game's story or come up with a **script** for game characters.

A developer at Electronic Arts makes changes to a character in the video game *MySims*.

Games with lots of characters and stories may need a **storyboard**. A storyboard is a series of drawings and writing that outlines a video game. It's like a comic book of the game.

Concept art, scripts, and storyboards are tools that help developers to plan. These tools help developers see the game in their minds before it is made. They know what kinds of challenges and levels to make when they begin the next stage of game creation.

Do the Math

Many computer game developers are interested in math. What's the connection? Both computer programs and math rely on logic. Logic is a way of problem solving that uses step-by-step methods to find solutions. People who study computers in school must take a lot of math classes as well. Mathematicians can also find work as game developers.

Programming

During programming, workers use computers to turn an idea into a game you can play. Programming a video game involves a lot of testing and making mistakes. Game developers must often rework the levels and challenges of a game.

A mistake in a program is called a **bug**. Bad bugs can make a game freeze up. They can even crash a computer. Programmers need to debug, or fix problems, in a game.

Game developers test games as they work. They want to figure out if parts of a game are too hard — or boring. They explore every part of their game. They try to think of everything a player might do. They must be sure that the game plays as they imagined it.

Games Get Serious

All games should be fun to play, but many designers hope their games provide more than just a good time. The makers of a game called *Food Force* wanted to teach players about hunger. They worked with the United Nations (UN) World Food Program. They learned how the UN helps starving people around the world. From there, they made storyboards and characters to reflect the UN's work. The project took months to complete.

On the Job: Game Designer Jonathan Blow

Jonathan Blow is a game designer. He worked for three years on the video game Braid.

Q: How did you get your start?

Blow: In the fifth grade, I had a class that taught introductory computer programming. Shortly after that, my parents bought me a computer at home because they saw how much I liked it. I have been doing computer stuff ever since.

Q: How did you come up with the idea for *Braid*?

Blow: [There isn't a process of] sitting down and thinking about what people will like or what people will buy. One day an idea appears to me, and it feels like something I really want to do.

Q: Did you know right away what the game would look like and play like?

Blow: *Braid* is a very complicated game. [There] are just a lot of ideas inside it. Because of that, a lot of ideas came later in development. [But] they all fit into ... the basic concept that I started with.

Q: Do you have any advice for an interested young person?

Blow: The most important thing is just to start making games, right now. Maybe it is something small at first, because you have never done it before and don't really know how. Then you use that experience to make something new, bigger, and better.

A scene from *Braid*

CHAPTER 3

WHO WORKS IN GAME DEVELOPMENT?

Small games might have two or even one person handling all the work. But big games may have dozens of people working on different parts of the project.

The most challenging video games are created by developers and programmers with special skills. Many have studied computers. Most employers prefer developers who have college degrees.

Game development offices are busy places full of activity.

Women at Work

About 40 percent of game players are girls and women. But most game programmers are men. Women hold only a small percentage of programming jobs. Some companies are now trying to bring in more women programmers. They hope that women programmers will help make more games that appeal to all kinds of fans.

Electronic Arts game developers accept a Guinness World Record for the game *Spore*.

Lead Programmer

Lead programmers direct the programming of a game. They are in charge of organizing the major ideas. When a project starts, the lead programmer may be one of a few people working on it. He or she may do a lot of programming. But as a project grows, lead programmers do more organizing. They figure out what kind of technology and people they need to make the game.

Lead programmers at big game companies have often worked in game development for many years. Their skills include more than just using a computer.

On the Job: A Lead Programmer

William Bryan began working at British game maker Rare right after college. He started as a junior programmer. He has worked there for more than 10 years. Bryan worked as the lead programmer on the *Viva Piñata* games for Xbox 360. When he started working on the games, he was the only programmer. Once the development was under way, he was in charge of a team of up to 60 people. "As the project progressed, my role became less hands-on coding and more decision making," he says.

They are also good at leading a team. They know how to manage the programmers that work for them. They also work with the company's business people.

Engine Programmer

Each game is a virtual world. Engine programmers create the rules for how that world works. They write software to control how objects move and affect other objects in the game. They may create programs to allow the game to run on different game systems.

All of this software together is called the game's engine. Game companies often use one **game engine** for several different games.

Programming requires a lot of time in front of computers!

Engine programmers must have a deep knowledge of computer programming. They know a lot about physical science and different kinds of technology. They may even have a doctorate in a particular area.

Tools Programmer

Many programmers use software written specially for a game. A tools programmer creates the software that is used by other workers on the team. The software helps other developers spend less time writing software and more time designing. Tools programmers must be good at creating programs that are easy for others to follow.

Graphics Programmer

Artists design much of the look of a game. Graphics programmers put that art into the game. Artists create drawings and three-dimensional, or 3-D, models in their computers. Graphics programmers write the software that brings the art to the screen.

Programmers make 3-D models in their computers. Then the models can move around on screen almost like in real life.

Graphics programmers might put a **skin** on 3-D models. Or they might create special effects for things such as smoke, explosions, or flowing water. This kind of programming requires a solid math background as well as an artistic eye.

Sound Programmer

Musicians, actors, and sound-effect artists help make all the sounds you hear in a game. Sound programmers write the software that produces the sound. They are usually familiar with the latest recording methods and sound mixing. They may study music and recording as well as computers in college.

AI Programmer

Artificial intelligence, or AI, programmers create the brains of a game's characters. They write the software that makes the creatures and people in games act as if they are real and alive. Today's games are pushing AI technology to new levels every year.

AI programmers must keep up with research in artificial intelligence. They are often interested in subjects such as **robotics** and biology as well as computers.

CHAPTER 4

THE TOOLS OF THE TRADE

You might play a video game on a special home system, a personal computer, or even your phone. No matter where a game ends up, it was programmed on a computer.

Game developers often study computers in school. Researchers in this field study everything from the mathematics of computing to robots. Game developers may also study **software engineering**. Software engineers focus on how to make software.

Learning computer programming in school is useful for students who want a job in video game programming. These students are familiar with many of the tools that game developers use every day.

Learning the Language

All game developers must be able to write software. To do that, they need to learn the **programming languages** of computers. A programming language is a set of words and rules that tell a computer what to do. There are thousands of programming languages but only a few in video game programming.

All video games are designed on computers. Even home console games such as *Guitar Hero World Tour* are designed on computers with development kits.

Some of the most common programming languages used to make video games are called C and C++. Different games use different programming languages. It depends on what system the game is for and which game engine is being used.

Computer Kits

The video games you play on a home system are created on a personal computer with a computer kit. Companies that make home systems, such as the Nintendo Wii or the Sony PlayStation, sell computer kits to game developers at other companies. The kits are a group of computer programs that help developers create a game to play on a home system.

Game developers can also buy their own software sets. They use these sets to make games on their computers. Flash is a popular set of software tools used for many games on the Internet. You can get some simple game development kits online for free. These kits can help people start making their own games as a hobby or even a business.

An owner of a video-gaming company teaches game design to a college student.

Working Without an Office

Ron Carmel (left) and Kyle Gabler (right) had what most game developers would call dream jobs. They worked at Electronic Arts, one of the world's biggest video game companies. But in 2006, they quit to form their own independent, or indie, company called 2D Boy. They released their first game, *World of Goo*, for the Nintendo Wii and personal computers in 2008. It had soon won awards for game of the year. That's pretty impressive for two developers who don't even have an office!

A scene from *World of Goo*

23

CHAPTER 5

MANY JOBS TO MAKE A GAME

Not everyone who works in video games started out in computer programming. Artists, writers, and businesspeople are just some of the people who work in this field.

Producers

Game developers may make the game, but someone needs to find ways to sell it. Producers connect the creative side with the business side.

Video game producers are in charge of managing the money needed to make a game. They hire the team for the project. Producers must have good leadership and management skills. Many have started out as developers and designers. They also come from the world of business. They may study business in college or graduate school. Producers are often some of the highest-paid members of a game development team.

Writers

Large video game companies often employ writers and editors. Some writers help to make the script for

Many creative minds spent many hours designing your favorite video games.

a game by writing stories for it. Scriptwriters are often hired after the idea for a game has been created.

Other writers produce the text in the instruction booklets and game web sites. All writers for games must be able to express themselves clearly. They also must be able to turn difficult technical information into clear, simple language. Video game writers often study English in college.

Designers and Artists

Artists are important parts of game development teams. They help create the look of the characters and the game world. Game companies will use many different artists to help them create a game. Some make drawings or 3-D models. Others **animate** the drawings to make them seem alive.

Game artists work closely with game designers. At small companies, they help shape a game's design. They create concept art and even write software. Large companies often hire artists who focus on one part of the design, such as making the characters. Artists who work for game companies may study art in college. Their job demands that they know a lot about computers as well.

Play Testers

Believe it or not, some people get paid to play video games. Game testing is one way to get started in the video game business. Game testers look for any bugs or other problems. Then they write reports about the problems for the development team.

Playing games for a living sounds like fun, but play testers are not paid as well as other game workers. They sometimes work long hours. Often, testers are hired for only a short period to test a game.

World Games

Some video game makers are now hiring workers from around the world to work on a single project. Most companies that hire workers from other countries use developers in China and India. The developers may all be working on the same game, but they are actually working in rooms thousands of miles apart.

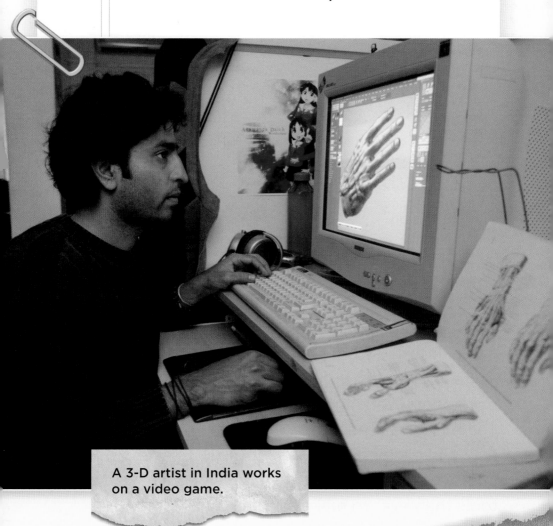

A 3-D artist in India works on a video game.

Would you like to get paid to play video games? That's what play testers do.

Game On!

There are many paths to a career in the video game industry, from play tester to programmer. Huge companies with thousands of employees and developers working in cafés put out all kinds of games. The business is huge and growing. Fans always demand new and exciting products. Computer technology improves each year. Creative developers have more tools than ever to make and sell their games.

VIDEO GAME DEVELOPER

OUTLOOK

- More than 24,000 people worked on video games and other entertainment software in the United States in 2006.

- The video game industry has been growing faster than other entertainment businesses in recent years. The U.S. government predicts that computer programming jobs will be one of the fastest growing parts of the economy from 2006 to 2016.

WHAT YOU'LL DO

- Video game developers write software for games that work on home consoles, handheld devices, personal computers, and arcade machines.

- Many different kinds of developers may work on a single game. Some are responsible for sound and graphics. Others create software to help other developers.

- Large companies often hire many developers to work on a single game. Small companies may have a few or even one developer working on a game.

WHAT YOU'LL NEED

- All developers must know a lot about computers. Game developers must also love video games. Many employers want workers who have studied programming in college.

- Developers must be able to spend long hours working at a computer.

WHAT YOU'LL EARN

- Beginning programming jobs often pay around $40,000 a year. Experienced workers earn more. The average pay for game developers is more than $70,000 a year.

Sources: U.S. Department of Labor, Bureau of Labor Statistics; Entertainment Software Association Annual Report; and *Game Developer*

GLOSSARY

animate — to make something seem alive

artificial intelligence — computer programs that carry out tasks that normally require human intelligence

bug — a mistake in a computer program

concept art — a form of illustration that shows the design or mood of a video game before it is used in the final product

engineers — people who design and build mechanical or electrical things

game engine — the main software that runs a video game

hardware — computer equipment

logic — a way of problem solving that uses step-by-step methods to find solutions

programming languages — defined sets of words and rules that tell a computer what to do

programs — series of instructions that tell computers or other machines what to do

robotics — the study and use of the technology of robots

script — the written part of a video game, including a description of the action as well as the dialogue

skin — a computer graphic that covers a 3-D model in a video game

software — the operating instructions and programs that a computer uses

software engineering — the study of the techniques of making software

storyboard — a series of drawings and writing that outlines a video game

video game developers — the artists, programmers, or producers who create video games

virtual — created by means of a computer

TO FIND OUT MORE

Books

Burns, Jan. *Shigeru Miyamoto: Nintendo Game Designer*. Detroit: KidHaven Press, 2006.

Cohen, Judith Love. *You Can Be a Woman Video Game Producer*. Marina del Rey, CA: Cascade Pass, 2006.

Duffield, Katy S. *Ken Kutaragi: PlayStation Developer*. Detroit: KidHaven Press, 2008.

Jozefowicz, Chris. *Video Games* (The Ultimate 10). Pleasantville, NY: Gareth Stevens, 2009.

Web Sites

Breaking In: Preparing for Your Career in Games
www.igda.org/breakingin
Learn about the different jobs for game developers, and get tips for getting started.

Entertainment Software Association
www.theesa.com
Explore facts and figures about the game industry.

**UN World Food Program: WFP Food Force—
The Game, The Reality, How to Help**
www.food-force.com
How do you play? What can you do to help? Find out more.

INDEX

About the Author

Chris Jozefowicz studied to be a scientist but ended up as a writer. He has written scientific papers, medical reports, news stories, magazine articles, and video game reviews. Today, he mainly writes articles about science. He lives with his wife and daughter in Louisville, Kentucky. He thanks all the game developers whose work has entertained him since he got his first Atari in 1980.